Sewing Skinner®
ULTRASUEDE® Fabric

by Pati Palmer and Susan Pletsch

cover and fashion illustrations ... Patty Andersen

technical artwork ... the authors

The purpose of this book is to give the "confidence to cut" into this beautiful and luxurious suede fabric.

Whenever brand names are mentioned, it is only to indicate to the consumer products we have personally tested and have been pleased with. We are not subsidized by anyone. There may very well be other products that are comparable or even better to aid you in your sewing or that may be developed after the printing of this book.

Many thanks to our friends for their help in editing the instructions for clarity and to Skinner® for developing so many wonderful fabrics that inspire the home sewer to develop her skills to the ultimate. Also, a special thanks to Marta McCoy Alto who has shared her vast experiences in developing and demonstrating Ultrasuede® fabric sewing techniques.

Published by Palmer/Pletsch Associates, Portland, Oregon U.S.A.

Printed by Paramount Printing and Lithographing Co., Inc., Portland, Oregon U.S.A.

Book inquiries may be sent to Palmer/Pletsch Associates, P.O. Box 8422, Portland, Oregon 97207.

ISBN 0-935278-01-X

About the authors . . . . . .

Pati Palmer and Susan Pletsch, two talented home economists,
have developed careers promoting a favorite hobby, home
sewing. They have co-authored four sewing books, have
established their own publishing company, and now travel
across the U.S. teaching seminars based on the Palmer/Pletsch
books. They also conduct textile and management seminars
with many fabric and department stores. Their most recent
accomplishments include designing patterns for Vogue Patterns,
and creating and starring in an educational film based on a
Palmer/Pletsch book.

Pati and Susan met as educational representatives for Armo
Co., a shaping fabrics manufacturer. Pati has been Corporate

Home Economist and
notions buyer for an
Oregon department
store. She graduated
from Oregon State Univ-
ersity with a B.S. in
Home Economics. She
is active in the American
Home Economics Asso-
ciation, Home Economists
in Business, and Fashion
Group.

Susan has been a home
economist with Talon
Consumer Education,
where she traveled extensively giving consumer programs
and teacher workshops. She was also a free-lance home
economist with many sewing related firms. Susan graduated
from Arizona State University in home economics and taught
home economics to special education students. She is active
in the American Home Economics Association and Home Economists in Business.

Pati and Susan are individually recognized for their sewing
skills and teaching and lecturing abilities. Together they
produce an unbeatable combination of knowledge, personality
and talent.

This is how we sew . . . . .

Our philosophy of sewing is that sewing should be fun, fast, and easy. Notice "painful" was not mentioned. You shouldn't have to pray over something for six months before you can wear it. But . . . we also believe in a professional look. There is no room in really fine sewing for the look of "loving hands at home". We have tried and found true all of the methods we are about to tell you for sewing Ultrasuede® fabric. Certainly there are other methods suitable to the fabric, but these are what we have found to be the fastest, easiest, and the most fun. We plan to go into depth and tell you everything we know about Ultrasuede® fabric and to hold your hand as you cut into this expensive yardage. Use this book as a combination reference manual and security blanket. You shall have the "confidence to cut"!

Table of Contents

Ultrasuede® Fabric... What Is It?

Ultrasuede® fabric -- the amazing new suede fabric that looks, feels, and sounds like suede, but functions like fabric. The only thing it doesn't do is to smell like suede -- a distinct plus! Made by a well-guarded process that took seven years to develop, this non-woven fabric is 60% polyester, 40% non-fibrous polyurethane.

Ultrasuede® fabric is the ultimate for the prestige - seeking home sewers who want to have a $300 designer dress or a $640 raincoat for one fourth the cost. We can save from $100 to $500 per garment in this luxurious fabric which has been used by very exclusive American fashion designers -- Halston, Bill Blass, and Anne Klein. We like to make the most of our sewing time -- that's why we sew with fabrics like Ultrasuede® . Everytime you make a garment from a special fabric or one with special detail or even use a designer pattern, you can multiply everything you put into it by the number seven and come up with the price of a comparable quality ready-made garment.

Ultrasuede® fabric has the fashion look of suede without any of the disadvantages. It is available in twenty colorfast colors unobtainable in real skins. Unlike real suede, it will not shrink, stretch, pill, fray, crock, or wrinkle. Unlike real suede, it will not waterspot or stiffen, can be cleaned by regular drycleaning methods, but most important, it can be machine washed and dried.

If this sounds like music to your ears, beware of one slightly discordant note -- it is an expensive fabric by any standards. It is over $40 per yard for a 45" wide fabric. But sweet sounds again -- remember it is an initial expense only. Even though it could cost you as much to make an Ultrasuede® fabric garment as it would a garment of real skin, there will never be those expensive leather cleaning bills. Are you excited? Read on -- then run out for supplies and start sewing on this lightweight, wrinkle resistant and seasonless fabric.

Pattern Selection

Let your imagination soar! Almost anything can be made from Ultrasuede® fabric -- we've seen a bikini (it seems to resist chlorine and be colorfast), a tablecloth (what a perfect gift for an affluent bachelor), handbags, shoes, belts, and any number of beautiful garments. Pati was even shopping in a Portland furniture store wearing her beautiful gold Ultrasuede® fabric skirt and looked to her side to find she was standing next to a chic sofa upholstered in the same color Ultrasuede® fabric. We've even made director's chair covers from Ultrasuede® fabric, and a friend patches her son's jeans with it. She says the patches wear well.

Remember its properties and take advantage of them:
1. It does not water spot or stiffen -- what could be more posh than a suede raincoat in a spring shower. Just spray with a water repellent product.

2. Lightweight and wrinkle resistant -- a perfectly packable pantsuit.

3. Machine washable -- an off-white suede blazer? You wouldn't dare in real suede!

4. Colorfast and crock resistant -- a suede belt that doesn't leave its color on your skirt nor stretch out of shape -- an easy first project in Ultrasuede® fabric.

5. Seasonless -- the fabric really has no season, so choose a garment you can wear year around for maximum enjoyment. It's amazingly durable. We may tire of our Ultrasuedes® long before they begin to give us a tired look in return.

Some basics:
1. Choose a simple pattern to show off this smashing fabric. For your first Ultrasuede® garment, consider

9

yourself a beginner again. Select one of the many good looking "jiffy" or "very easy" pattern, perhaps a simple wrap jacket or an easy little vest. Then graduate to something more intricate after you've gained confidence.

2. Select a pattern with minimum easing since Ultrasuede® fabric like real suede will ease only 1" in 10". However set-in sleeves are definitely possible with tricks we will show you later. Some great looking alternatives to set-in sleeves are kimono, raglan, dropped shoulder, and sleeveless.

3. Yoked or seamed pants and skirts are better than those with waist darts. It is hard to get such short darts to lie flat and smooth. They tend to bubble.

4. If you are larger than a "C" bra cup size, choose a pattern with bust darts or vertical over-the-bust seams. (For information on how to add a bust dart to a pattern that doesn't have one see page 85 in Mother Pletsch's Painless Sewing. Ordering information on page 79 of this book.)

5. Avoid "For Knits Only" patterns with Ultrasuede® fabric. They rely on the fabric stretching for comfort and fit. Ultrasuede® has no more give than a woven fabric.

6. Don't get hungup on the "classic shirtdress" look. It is nice and can be worn many ways, but consider a jumper, skirt, culottes, vest, tunic, zip front jacket, blazer and dresses with square armholes.

7. Ultrasuede® can be gathered nicely as gathers below a yoke or a shirred waist jacket -- but it will add a little bulk, so decide if you can tolerate the larger illusion. We have seen beautiful soft skirts slightly gathered at the waist and coats with full backs gathered to a yoke and pulled in with a belt at the waist.

10

How Much Yardage to Buy?

This is our most frequently asked question and we wish we could give you a magic formula -- but unfortunately there is none. You can be safe and buy the amount of fabric the pattern suggests for a 45" "with nap" fabric and then use any extra fabric for trimming another garment or for making patchwork. Or -- you can do some preplanning and then purchase exactly the amount your pattern, in your size, with your choice of seams, will require. We have found that preplanning can save from $5.00 to $50.00 in Ultrasuede®!!

Follow these steps to save fabric:

1. Read the entire book first! We mention many fabric saving ideas throughout the book.

2. Select and purchase your pattern.

3. Determine the construction method you want to use.

4. Conventional method: Buy fabric according to pattern directions, using the 45" "with nap" yardage requirement.

5. Flat Method:
   - Trim 5/8" seam allowances and hem allowances off tissue paper pattern where necessary. (Guidelines are given on page 30.)
   - Lay out trimmed tissue pattern on a premarked cutting board to find out exactly how much yardage you'll need.
   - Now because you have snipped away unnecessary hem and seam allowances, your pattern pieces will be much smaller and will fit into a smaller space. This allows you to buy less Ultrasuede yardage than the pattern called for.

NOTE: Marta suggests: Buy a 3 yard piece of gingham to use for trial pattern layouts for any fabric over $5.00 a yard. Gingham has built-in grainline markings. Fold it to the width of your fabric being purchased and do a compact pattern layout.

Suitable Shaping Fabrics

INTERFACINGS

Interfacings are a must in almost every garment.

1. They are used to give strength and to prevent stretch on the edges that get wear - neck, front and cuff.

2. Garments wear better when interfaced in stress areas such as under buttons and buttonholes.

3. Interfacings give shape and body to detail areas - collars, pocket flaps and belts.

4. With Ultrasuede® fabric, we had the best results with fusible interfacings , the interfacings that are steam-pressed to the fabric and require no tailoring knowledge.

There seems to be some controversy as to shaping Ultrasuede® fabric or not. We find that because Ultrasuede® is a fabric with more body, we generally use lighter weight interfacings. But the garments with interfacings in the proper places will look better than those without. A collar has more body, a band doesn't pucker, and a machine buttonhole won't ripple with an interfacing inside.

FUSIBLES VERSUS IRON-ONS

We love the new fusibles with Ultrasuede® -- we don't use anything else. If you've been wary of fusibles because of past poor performance from the "iron-on" products, be wary no more. The old "iron-ons" were fabrics backed with flakey granules that fell off before you got them home. The new fusibles have a fusing agentspread smoothly and evenly on the back of the fabric by a calendering method or a computer dot method. With the old "iron-ons" you used only heat and pressure. The new "fusibles" require <u>steam</u>, heat, and pressure.

Today's fusibles will:
1. Machine wash and dry
2. Dry clean
3. Last the life of the garment
4. Be suitable for even heat sensitive fabrics

TYPES OF FUSIBLES - Always make a test sample first!

The following categories of fusible interfacings are suggested:

1. Heavy - Fusible Acro (woven) is the only washable hair canvas and is great for the extra body needed in a coat or blazer. It is very resilient and gives a somewhat firm shape for a well-tailored look. Heavyweight Pel-Aire from Pellon is an excellent new non-woven interfacing designed for tailoring.

2. Medium - Armo-Weft (woven), Mid-Weight Fusible Pellon, Easy Shaper Suit Weight, and mediumweight Pel-Aire from Pellon, (all non-wovens) are a little lighter and used to create a less firm appearance. We usually choose medium-weight interfacings for most of our Ultrasuede sewing.

3. Light - Fusible Featherweight Pellon and Easy Shaper Light Weight (non-wovens) and Easy Knit (knit) are great where just a touch of body is desired, such as in a collarless neckline, a vest, or wrap-front dress or jacket.

4. Fusible Webs - Pellon Fusible Web, Magic Polyweb, and Stitch Witchery are all independent fusing agents used to fuse Ultrasuede® fabric to itself or to temporarily "steam baste" two layers of Ultrasuede® together (see page 29). They are great for holding a patch pocket in place before stitching (page 68) or for holding a lapped seam in place and preventing slippage during topstitching (page 28).

NOTE: Be sure to read the complete instructions for preshrinking fusible interfacings on page 19.   DO NOT preshrink fusible web.

HOW TO FUSE

It is extremely important to fuse properly. You must use a minimum of 10 seconds for lightweight fusibles and 15 seconds for heavyweight fusibles. 10 seconds is longer than you think. Susan uses the Mississippi trick: one Mississippi, two Mississippi, three Mississippi, etc. You will then be sure to fuse for a full 10 seconds.

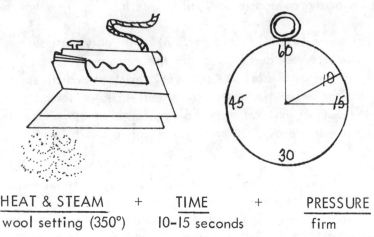

HEAT & STEAM	+	TIME	+	PRESSURE
wool setting (350°)		10-15 seconds		firm

UNDERLINING

An underlining is a separate layer of fabric attached to the wrong side of each piece of your fashion fabric and included in all the seams. It is used to give additional body and strength in some areas. We advise underlining pants especially in the crotch seam. We have seen Ultrasuede® tear away from the stitching line, even when twill tape was sewed in for strength. Protect that Ultrasuede.® It is better to put the stress on the underlining. Men seem to be harder on pants so we have included these instructions on page 76 in the "Sewing Menswear" chapter, however, we recommend an underlining in women's pants also. An additional plus is that the underlined pants won't stick to your legs.

Try Poly-SiBonne (ideal because it breathes and is easy to handle) or an all polyester lining fabric like the lightweight ones suggested in the lining section.

LINING

A lining is assembled separately and used to finish the inside of a garment. You may want to line Ultrasuede®since it is not at all slippery. It's very hard to slip into a jacket when your sweater is sticking to the sleeves.

Some things to consider:
1. A lining can be a fashion plus for the garment. Coordinate a super print or a contrasting color to your Ultrasuede®.

2. Select a lining with the same characteristics as Ultrasuede® (machine washable and dryable, no pressing needed, and very durable). Any medium to lightweight woven fabric with a slightly slick surface is suitable.

   AlaCreme or Noblesse – woven fabrics by Skinner,® makers of Ultrasuede®, that are dyed to match Ultrasuede. They are 100% polyester, lightweight, beautifully silky, and great for blouses and dresses.

   Lutesong – a woven polyester satin by Skinner® in yummy colors that coordinate with Ultrasuede®. It is heavier than the other suggestions and great as a coat lining.

   Coupe de Ville – a woven fabric by Burlington/Klopman that is all polyester and silky. It is available in solids and prints.

   Qiana®– a duPont nylon fiber with the look and feel of silk. Woven Qiana fabrics are great linings for Ultrasuede®as they breathe and are comfortable to wear.

Where to line:
   Sleeves – Always! Most Ultrasuede®garments are worn over other things–sleeves will slip on more easily when lined.

   Coats and blazers – need a lining to cover the inner construction, and are easier to slip on over other garments.

   Shirtjackets and shirtdresses – you may want to line the sleeves and possibly the yoke for greater ease in slipping on and off.

   Vests – optional.

   Skirts – optional.

Helpful Notions

Gadgets or conveniences??? Sometimes a great notion can make life very simple. How many kitchen gadgets have you purchased over the years? Could you live without an egg beater, a rolling pin, egg slicer, a blender, a meat thermometer, a dial timer or paper towels? Certainly you could--- but don't they make life in the kitchen more tolerable? Notions can do the same in the sewing room.

The following notions are particularly helpful with Ultrasuede® fabric:

✓ 1. Talon Basting Tape®--a double-faced sewing tape used in place of pins or hand basting. A tremendous time-saver !

2. Fusible web--Pellon Fusible Web®, Magic Polyweb®, or Stitch Witchery® You'll need one yard or several packages of the precut strips. This is a must in sewing Ultrasuede® fabric.

3. Tri-Shape (Stacy) or Ti-Rite (Armo)--washable rayon and polyester woven lambswool-like interfacing and under-lining fabrics. They are used to help set in sleeves and to shape the sleeve cap - you need to buy 3/8 yard.

✓ 4. Thread--choose a lightweight 100% polyester or a polyester core thread. We also like the fineness of pure silk thread. For topstitching the easiest is one strand of polyester thread. If you want the thread to be more obvious, run two strands of polyester thread through a size 16 needle. Do a test sample always.

5. Topstitching thread--silk buttonhole twist or one of the new polyester topstitching threads are heavier, more lustrous, and more easily visible than regular thread. We use regular thread in the bobbin and topstitching thread on top and a size 16 or 18 needle. If you get skipped stitches with this type of thread try one of the following: use topstitching thread in the bobbin instead; use it in both bobbin and on top; make sure your needle is sharp; you may not be able to sew through two layers of Ultrasuede unless they are fused together; or try the "Yellow Band" needle.

6. Machine needles--it is essential to make only fine holes in Ultrasuede® fabric to prevent weakening it, so use a size 11/12 or even a size 9/10. Do a test sample. You may need a size 16 with silk or polyester buttonhole twist. We found no difference between ballpoint and sharp needles.

7. Singer "Yellow Band" sewing machine needles--a real sanity saver if your machine has a tendency to skip stitches. Because of a unique design, Yellow Band ball point needle will prevent skipped stitches on Ultrasuede and other firm finished fabrics. Now available in sizes 11, 14, and 16, it's super for all seam stitching and topstitching.

8. Hand sewing needles--the finer the better. A size 10 sharp moves easily through the firm fabric. Since Ultrasuede® is such a tough fabric, a thimble is a necessity for hand sewing.

9. Pins--look for "easy-on-the-fingers" glass or plastic head pins - fine, long ones are best.

10. Zippers--choose a nylon or polyester coil zipper as they are much stronger than metal and more compatible with the fabric than a metal zipper. Be sure to preshrink if they are not marked "low shrink".

11. Shears--select a pair that is very sharp and has a bent handle so the fabric will lie flat when cutting. Be sure to have your shears sharpened before cutting Ultarsuede®, since a clean-cut edge is essential. Better yet, treat yourself to a new pair.

12. Marking equipment--a smooth-edged tracing wheel and paper, marking chalk or paper, or a lead pencil. They are all handy.

13. Press cloth--the sheer, see-through type will be easy to use. Cheesecloth is v.g.

14. Pressing equipment--pressing ham, seam roll, point presser/pounding block, white vinegar, and the June Tailor Board for pressing collars, curves and points.

15. Steam iron--we like the "Shot of Steam" or "Surge of Steam" irons. Pressing goes more quickly.

16. Hot-iron cleaner--such as Stacy's Clean & Glide or Iron-Off by Dritz - the easy way to clean or remove fusing agents from your iron soleplate.

17. The Steamstress--a "steam only" steamer. Because the steamstress has a cool plastic soleplate, it can be used to top-press Ultrasuede , velvet, and dark wools without creating shine or flattening the nap and eliminates the need for a press cloth. Trust the directions - use the recommended table salt for maximum steam. This should not be used to permanently fuse.

18. X-Acto Knife--a super sharp craft tool that's great for slicing open buttonholes. Look in a craft or hobby shop - be sure to buy extra blades.

19. Scotch Magic Transparent Tape®--used to denote right from wrong side, to mark seam allowances or stitching lines.

20. Belding Corticelli's Tape Stitch--a premarked tape used for a topstitching guideline.

NOTE: Be sure to remove any tapes from Ultrasuede® fabric with the direction of the nap.

21. Sobo Glue--a fabric glue that's great for attaching underlining to fashion fabric.

Fabric Preparation

PRESHRINKING

1. Ultrasuede® fabric -- not necessary. In testing, there seems to be no noticeable shrinkage. If you wish to preshrink, see care instructions on page 78.

2. Things that go with Ultrasuede® fabric -- necessary, unless you have purchased 100% polyester items.

   zippers---if they are not the low shrink type, put them in a basin of hot water until it cools and allow to air dry or run through a load of clothes in the washer and dryer. Be sure zippers are closed at all times when running them through the washer and dryer--zip up! To further protect zipper, place in a mesh hosiery bag or an old nylon stocking.

   twill tape---(used to tape roll line in blazers)--bend packaging card and stand in basin of hot water until it cools. The bend in the card gives it shrinking room and keeps the tape neat. Stand on edge to dry.

   fusible interfacings---WOVEN fusibles are the only ones that need preshrinking. The fusing granules are not water soluble. Carefully place interfacings into a basin of hot water for 10 minutes. Allow to dry flat on a towel. DO NOT WRING. The granules may come loose.

19

NOTE: Do not preshrink fusibles of any type in your washer or dryer as the granules may come loose. DO NOT preshrink fusible web.

NOTE: NON-WOVEN fusibles do not need regular pre-shrinking, but may need "steam shrinking." Place the interfacing on your fabric and steam with the iron 1" above it, then fuse the interfacing in place.

linings and underlinings---preshrink by machine washing and drying. It is so easy. Why take a chance? Some polyester linings hardly shrink, but others do shrink noticeably.

skirt - center back zipper or pocket closure

Pattern Fitting

FIT PATTERN BEFORE YOU CUT

There are four good ways to be safe:

1. Make a felt or Pellon shell -- we recommend making a complete shell so you are sure of the amount of ease you will have. Felt and Pellon hang like Ultrasuede® and will give you a good idea of the look and fit of your pattern.

2. Use a pattern you have used before on a woven fabric -- (a smart move!) Try on the previous garment to recheck the fit. Hopefully, you had marked any alterations made on this garment on your pattern. Make sure you are wearing the same undergarments or garments that you plan to wear with your Ultrasuede® fabric garment.

3. Pin the paper pattern pieces together and try them on-- the paper pattern will hang like Ultrasuede®. This is our favorite method because it's speedy and we can also check the style quickly and see how it looks on us.

4. Flat pattern measure -- measure all pattern pieces as shown and compare to your own body measurements.

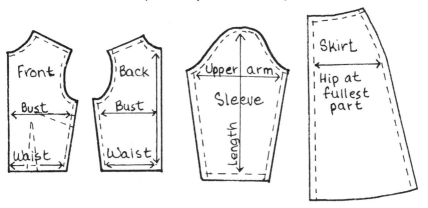

For complete instructions on fitting bodices, skirts and dresses, refer to our book Mother Pletsch's Painless Sewing and for pants to Pants For Any Body, revised edition. (Ordering information on page 80 .)

21

EASE

Purchase your usual pattern size, but be sure you allow adequate ease in your Ultrasuede® garment. Your pattern should be larger than your body by the amounts suggested in the chart below. There are two types of ease built into patterns – fitting ease and design ease. Pattern companies try to give you enough ease to be comfortable (fitting ease), but a designer can add or take away from the standard in order to create the look he or she wants (design ease). The only way you'll know how much ease there is in a pattern is to measure it.

You should allow enough ease to move. We recommend AT LEAST the following amounts for Ultrasuede®:

	DRESSES	COATS
BUST	2 - 3"	4 - 5"
WAIST	0 - 3/4"	depends on style
HIP	2"	2 - 4"
UPPER ARM	2 - 3"	4 - 5"
BACK WAIST LENGTH	1/4 - 1/2"	1/4 - 1/2"

NOTE: Vogue alerts us that if a coat is shown on the pattern envelope over a blouse only, then it only has enough ease to be worn over a blouse or lightweight dress. It can be worn over a heavy sweater or another jacket ONLY if shown that way. AN EXCELLENT POINT! For more excellent information you might refer to a back issue of Vogue Pattern Magazine May/June 1974 page 56. It also refers to ease allowed in various styles.

FIT GARMENT AFTER YOU CUT

1. The "pin and chalk" method – pin the entire garment together exactly as you would sew it with pins parallel to the cut edges. Don't worry about pin holes showing as they will disappear later in pressing. Try the garment on and repin until you get a smooth fit. Use tailor's chalk and mark the seamline or the lapping line depending on which construction method you are using.

2. The "steam baste" method – used to fit the flat method only. See page 29 for directions.

Which Construction Method?

There are 3 construction methods which may be used on Ultrasuede® fabric:

Conventional Method

Flat Method

Combination Method

There are no definite guidelines as to which method to use. It is personal preference. Designers are currently using all three methods. The flat seems to be the easiest for beginners, but gives a lot sportier appearance due to all of the topstitching. See the fashion illustration at heading of this chapter for a comparison between the flat and conventional look.

CONVENTIONAL METHOD

This method is used to create a classic or dressy appearance in a suede garment. It does require special sewing and pressing techniques in order to get a professional look.

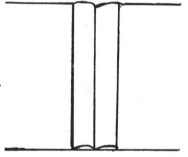

Characteristics of garments made using this method:
1. 5/8" seams, stitched and pressed open.
2. Collar and facing edges have enclosed seams.
3. Turned up hems (fused or hand stitched).
4. Lining is almost essential since inside is unfinished.
5. Little or no top stitching.

NOTE: Follow the sequence of construction on your pattern guide sheet, because the conventional method treats Ultrasuede® fabric like any other fabric.

Seams - conventional method

1. Hold seams together for sewing by using:

   - Fine pins placed in the seam allowances only.

   - Talon Basting Tape -- a double-faced tape. It not
     only holds the seam allowances together, but prevents
     fabric from slipping.

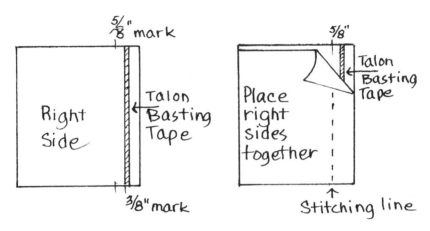

Place tape 3/8" from edge and
remove protective paper.

Stick seam allowances
right sides together.

2. Stitch at 5/8" seamline using 10 - 12 stitches per inch.

NOTE: Sewing seams in any modern fabric can cause diffi-
culties such as puckering or slippage. However, if you use the
"TAUT SEWING TECHNIQUE," you can easily handle almost
any fabric by just pulling equally on your fabric in front of and
behind the needle as you sew. Do not stretch, just pull until
taut. It is the fastest way of helping fabrics feed through the
machine evenly and preventing puckered seams.

3. Gently pull seam allowances apart and remove
   basting tape. Press
   open over seam roll with
   iron and flatten with
   wooden clapper.

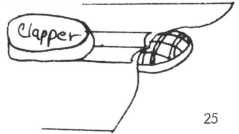

25

Flatten seams - 3 additional methods.

1. Slip strips of fusible web under each side of seam allowances and press flat.

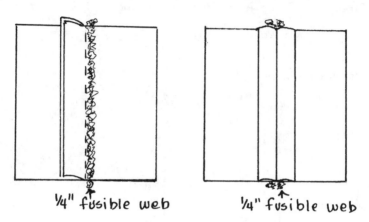

¼" fusible web   ¼" fusible web

2. Topstitch both seam allowances flat or to one side.

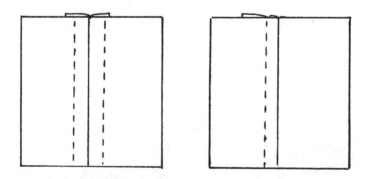

NOTE: TAKE YOUR TIME - don't rush!
Sew and press several test samples to become familiar with the fabric.

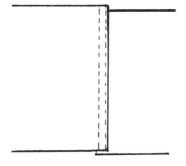

FLAT METHOD

This method is used for a flat sporty appearance. It also uses less fabric.

Characteristics of garments made using this method:

1. All seams are lapped and topstitched. Trim one seam away entirely when cutting.
2. All faced outer edges have no seam allowances (collars, lapels, front edge and neck without collar).
3. All hems are raw edges with or without a facing.
4. Since there is a clean finished look inside, lining is optional.
5. Pockets, tabs and flaps have no seam allowances.

NOTE: There is lots of topstitching, but even if you don't sew perfectly straight, your slightly wiggly lines will generally blend into the nap.

NOTE: Since you do so much topstitching with the flat method be sure to pull all threads through to wrong side and tie. A neat way to hide thread ends is to re-thread ends through a large needle and take a stitch between 2 layers of Ultrasuede® and come out in an inconspicuous place. When you can't bury the threads (such as in a single layer) use a dot of Sobo glue on your knot. Sobo is not water soluble so your knot will never ravel out.

First line of stitching furthest from seamline.
Lap front over back.

Seams using the flat method.

1. Trim 5/8" off overlap side (A). Leave full 5/8" on underlap side (B).

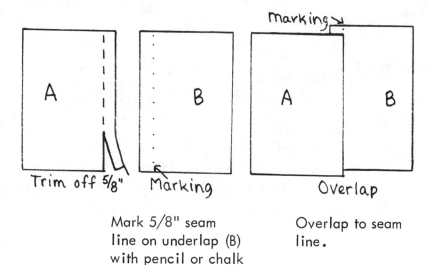

Trim off 5/8"   Marking   Overlap

Mark 5/8" seam line on underlap (B) with pencil or chalk on right side.   Overlap to seam line.

2. Slip a 1/4" wide strip of fusible web between the layers and steam base in place. Topstitch 1/4" away from seam line and again next to edge.

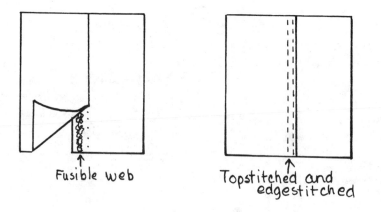

Fusible web   Topstitched and edgestitched

NOTE: "Steam basting" is a neat trick. It is a way to hold seams together for top-stitching. AND, for fitting, you can EVEN try on a whole garment that is only "steam basted" together. Place fusible web between fabrics, press lightly with a steam iron and press cloth for 2-3 seconds only. This will barely hold or baste the layers together. If you make a mistake - you can easily separate the layers, scratch away the unmelted web and re-fuse.

A HANDY TRICK:

You'll be using a lot of fusible web in narrow 1/4" strips, so buy it by the yard--- it's less expensive---and cut your own strips. To save hours of time, fold a yard of fusible fusible web into 8 or more folds and cut through all thicknesses.

PREPARING PATTERN FOR FLAT METHOD

Trim or fold back seam allowances on <u>tissue paper pattern</u> in amount indicated on the following edges: (Be sure to re-mark notches on 5/8" seam line before trimming.)

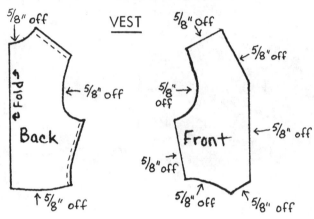

SHIRTDRESS (JACKET) WITH FRONT AND COLLAR BANDS

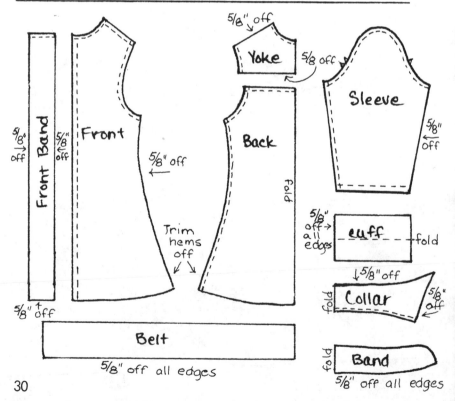

BLAZER

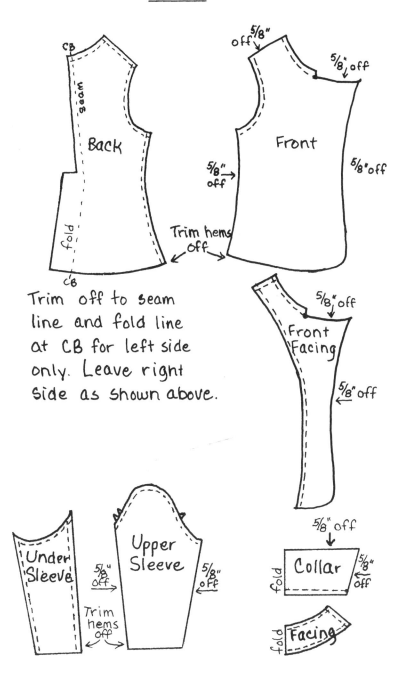

CB

seam

Back

fold

CB

off ⁵⁄₈"

⁵⁄₈" off

Front

⁵⁄₈" off

⁵⁄₈" off

⁵⁄₈" off

Trim hems off

Trim off to seam line and fold line at CB for left side only. Leave right side as shown above.

⁵⁄₈" off

Front Facing

⁵⁄₈" off

⁵⁄₈" off

Under Sleeve

⁵⁄₈" off

Upper Sleeve

⁵⁄₈" off

Trim hems off

fold

Collar

⁵⁄₈" off

fold

Facing

SKIRT

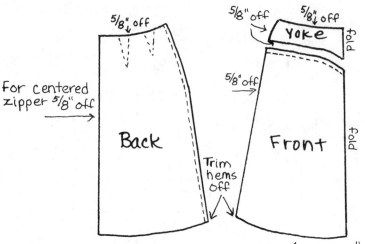

5/8" off
5/8" off
5/8" off
yoke
fold

For centered
zipper 5/8" off

5/8" off

Back

Front

fold

Trim
hems
off

For lapped zipper, see "Zippers" p. 56
For waist, see "Waistlines" p. 58

PANTS WITH FLY FRONT

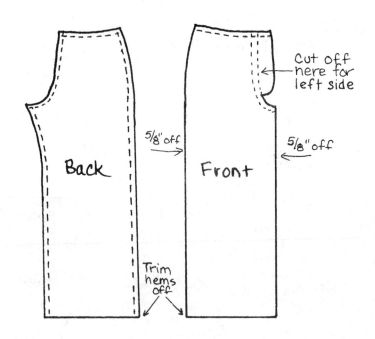

Cut off
here for
left side

5/8" off

5/8" off

Back

Front

Trim
hems

COMBINATION METHOD

There are times when sewing will be easier and the garment will be more comfortable to wear if you combine conventional and flat methods.

In any garment, we prefer to sew the following seams conventionally:

1. Set-in sleeve seam – It is easier to sew a set-in sleeve conventionally, the appearance is better, and you get greater wearing comfort.

2. Convertible collar to neckline seam – we prefer the clean appearance, especially in a blazer where it really shows.

conventional seams

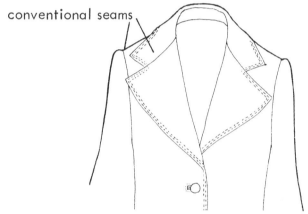

3. Pant crotch seam – it is much more comfortable to have a conventional crotch seam than a flat one – Susan knows.

You may also want to try conventional seams in these areas even if the rest of your garment is done flat method:

1. Sleeve underarm seam – for speed! It takes more time and talent to sew a flat seam inside a tube.

2. Pant inseam – again because it is faster and allows you to avoid sewing in a tube.

NOTE: Pati suggests sewing pant outseams conventionally for easier fitting. If your weight tends to fluctuate, this also allows more room for alterations AND they are much easier to alter.

As well as combining methods, you can easily change design. It's easy to add a seam or a detail in Ultrasuede® especially when using the flat method as shown below.

DESIGNING YOUR OWN WESTERN CUT PANTS

(begin with a good fitting basic pattern)

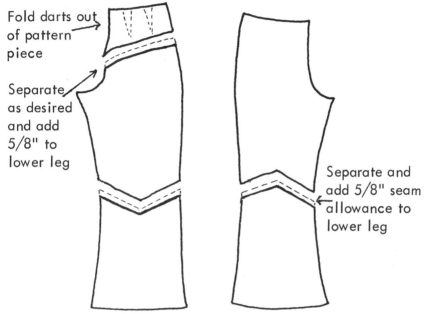

Fold darts out of pattern piece

Separate as desired and add 5/8" to lower leg

Separate and add 5/8" seam allowance to lower leg

CONVERTING DARTS IN PANTS TO SEAMS

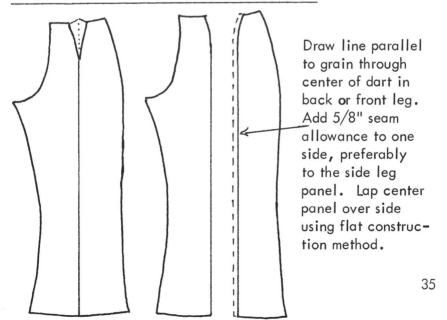

Draw line parallel to grain through center of dart in back or front leg. Add 5/8" seam allowance to one side, preferably to the side leg panel. Lap center panel over side using flat construction method.

35

Pattern Layout

ULTRASUEDE, LIKE REAL SUEDE, HAS A NAP

1. Cut with nap running up for a richer darker look.

2. Cut with nap running down for a lighter shinier look.

3. Or, for a real suede look, with shading, cut the pieces at random using both nap directions. Even if you do adhere to one direction, you may tilt the pattern pieces if necessary to get better mileage in cutting.

ULTRASUEDE IS A NON-WOVEN FABRIC, BUT IT HAS DIRECTIONAL DIFFERENCES

1. We tested the crosswise, lengthwise and bias directions for stretch and found the crosswise and bias stretch to be similar and the lengthwise direction to stretch the least. Bias collars and cuffs, for example, may be cut on the crosswise to save fabric.

2. Crosswise direction will be the most comfortable, so place it going around the body for comfort give.

3. Pattern pieces tilted or cut "off grain" in order to save fabric will not harm fabric drape.

ULTRASUEDE MAY EASILY BE CUT DOUBLE FOR SPEED

1. Fold the fabric with the right sides outside, wrong sides together for quicker marking.

2. Place a small strip (1" in length) of Talon Basting Tape along edge between the layers every 12" to keep the fabric from shifting.

3. Use glass-head pins pushed vertically through the fabric into the cutting board. Try to keep pins in seam allowances. However, pinholes disappear when fabric is steamed.

6 Ways To Save Fabric

1. Choose patterns that have lots of seams. Little pieces can be squeezed into unbelievable spaces.

2. Use the flat method of construction. For example, leaving the hem off a skirt may save $5.00.

3. Lay out your pattern pieces before you buy your Ultrasuede® to determine exactly how much yardage you need.

4. Tilt pattern pieces. They may be tilted up to a 45 degree angle without a noticeable color difference.

5. Separate cut-on facings if necessary.

6. Cut through a single layer of Ultrasuede® if necessary. (Ugh!)

Cutting Tips

1. Before cutting decide on your sewing method. Trim or fold back seam allowances on pattern where necessary if using flat method.

2. See the zipper section, decide on method of application, and trim seams off pattern where indicated.

3. Cut with fabric folded wrong sides together for easier marking later. Use long, bent handled shears with steady even slashes. Keep one hand flat on the edges of the pattern pieces while cutting.

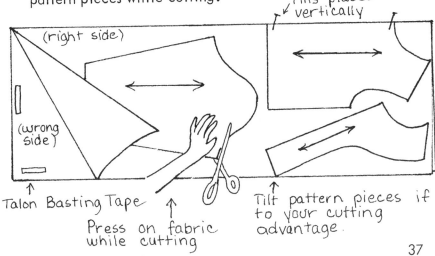

Pins placed vertically

(right side)

(wrong side)

Talon Basting Tape

Press on fabric while cutting

Tilt pattern pieces if to your cutting advantage.

37

Marking Helps

1. You can use a soft lead or chalk pencil on the wrong side. It brushes away and is particularly good on unlined garments.

2. You may also use washable tracing paper and a smooth edge tracing wheel to mark on Ultrasuede® fabric.

3. When cutting double, put pins through the dart points vertically and lift up top layer of Ultrasuede® fabric. Mark with pencil or chalk at point where pin is penetrating fabric. Connect dots with a ruler if you like.

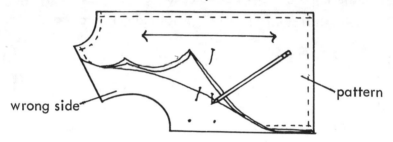

wrong side

pattern

4. If you are using the flat method, try these special helps:

Transfer notches with pencil mark just inside seam line on pattern before cutting away seam allowance on overlap side. After cutting Ultrasuede®, transfer marks to wrong side at edges with chalk or pencil.

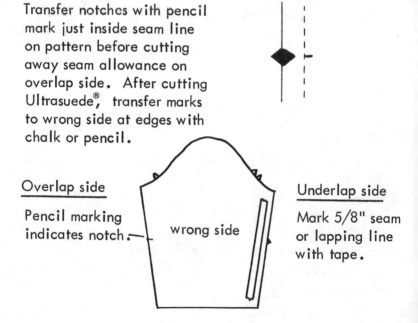

Overlap side

Pencil marking indicates notch.

wrong side

Underlap side

Mark 5/8" seam or lapping line with tape.

Darts

CONVENTIONAL DARTS

We recommend this method as it is stronger and smoother. After all, you don't always want to emphasis your darts.

1. Fuse a 1" circle of fusible interfacing over dart point. This will prevent a pucker at point of dart. *After sewn*

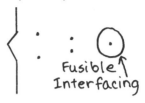
Fusible Interfacing

2. Stitch dart to a very fine, tapered point through fusible interfacing.

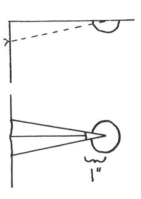

3. Slash the dart to within 1" of the point. Press open. Slip strips of brown paper under the dart edges to keep them from leaving an imprint on the right side.

1"

NOTE: Avoid a puckered dart by changing to smaller stitches 1/2" from point. Your machine will go slower, giving you more control. The last four stitches should be on the very edge. To knot, stitch off end several times creating a chain. Pull dart forward, knotting in place in seam allowance of dart.

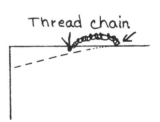
Thread chain

FLAT METHOD DARTS: Cut vertical darts on stitching line closest to center front or center back, and horizontal darts from the top stitching line to the point. Lap seam lines, steam baste, topstitch. To reinforce the point fuse a small circle of Ultrasuede over the point on wrong side before topstitching, or hide the point with a patch pocket! Make test sample first.

Press As You Sew

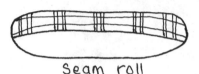

Seam roll

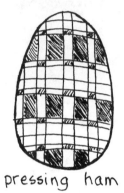

pressing ham

pounding block

Steam iron

1. Press _as_ you sew.
2. Use lots of steam.
3. Use a synthetic setting.
4. Press on the wrong side using a press cloth. However, with a wool flannel or Ultrasuede® press cloth or a Steam-stress, you may press on the right side.
5. Press seams over a seam roll to avoid seam imprint on right side.
6. To get nice flat seams, use a pounding block. (Put strips of paper under seam allowances to prevent an imprint on the right side.)
7. If seams won't press flat use a press cloth dipped in a solution of 1 T. white vinegar and a cup of water.
8. If you get an iron imprint from too much pressure, restore nap with steam and by brushing with a toothbrush.
9. Use a pressing ham to shape darts and curved seams.
10. If a seam has been ripped out, remove needle holes by steam pressing and brushing with a toothbrush.

Never ease More Than 1" — Measure before cutting [Abstretchove 1/2" pattern] from most patterns

Necessary Details: Sleeves and Collars

SETTING IN A SLEEVE

Sleeves should be set in conventionally, even in a flat method garment. The sound of the term "setting in a sleeve" often makes the strongest soul quake---and it shouldn't. Read on to find out about a great new way to get a PUCKER FREE set-in sleeve in Ultrasuede®or any other fabric...

1. Purchase 3/8 yd. of Ti-Rite or Tri-Shape interfacing. Cut a bias strip 12" long and 1 1/2" wide for each sleeve. Place strip on wrong side of sleeve cap lining up top edges. Sew to sleeve cap just a hair less than 5/8" stitching line stretching bias to fullest degree while sewing.

2. VOILA! Sleeve cap is automatically eased and ready to sew into garment armhole. (Even if the sleeve is still a bit large for the armhol it will be easier to get the additional ease in smoothly.)

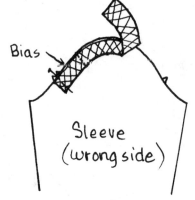

Bias

Sleeve
(wrong side)

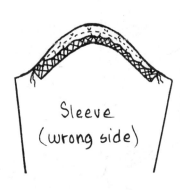

Sleeve
(wrong side)

3. Pin and stitch sleeve into jacket armhole. Smooth ease with fingers after stitching.

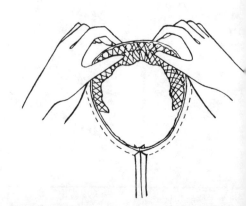

42

4. Trim cap to 1/4".

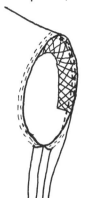

5. Always press sleeve cap from the Inside.

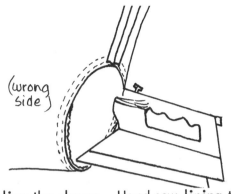

(wrong side)

6. To hide the Tri-Shape, line the sleeve. Hand sew lining to sleeve cap. Lining will force Tri-Shape into sleeve cap, giving the cap a nice smooth padded look.

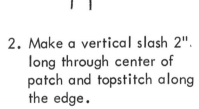

Turn under 3/8" on lining cap and sew to sleeve seam line of garment. (Sew a line of stitching on lining seam first to make it easier to turn.)

PLACKETS

1. Make placket if sleeve has a cuff. Fuse a 2 1/2" by 1 1/2" rectangle of Ultra-suede®, wrong sides together over the placket area. (Cut rectangle of fusible web slightly smaller to avoid ridges of patch from showing on outside.

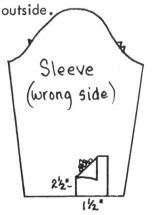

Sleeve (wrong side)

2 1/2"

1 1/2"

2. Make a vertical slash 2" long through center of patch and topstitch along the edge.

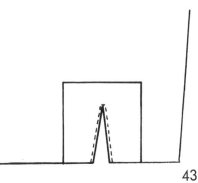

take in here

slash

SLEEVE LININGS

1. Sew underarm seam in lining.

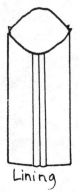

Lining

2. Sew underarm seam in sleeve.

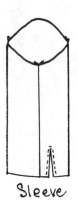

Sleeve

3. Drop lining into sleeve and machine baste together at bottom. (Use 2 rows of stitching if you will be gathering sleeve to cuff.)

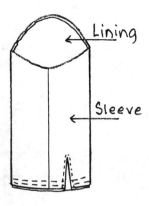

Lining

Sleeve

4. Make a 2 1/4" vertical slash in lining at placket opening. Turn under and hand stitch or machine topstitch to placket facing.

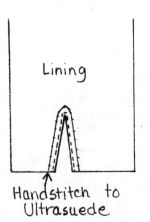

Lining

Handstitch to Ultrasuede

CUFFS --- FLAT METHOD
(for conventional cuff, follow pattern directions)

1. Trim seam allowances off all cuff edges. Trim interfacing 1/4" smaller than cuff. Fuse interfacing to <u>upper</u> cuff.

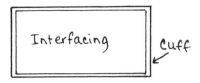

Interfacing

Cuff

2. Steam baste upper cuff to outside of sleeve seam allowance and under cuff to lining side. Steam baste all outside edges together.

3. Topstitch 2 rows around entire cuff.

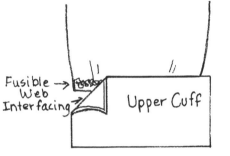

Fusible Web Interfacing

Upper Cuff

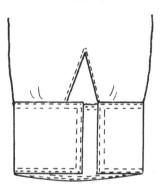

NOTE: Look for a pattern with a <u>side back seam</u>. They are super simple to sew because you can attach the cuff while the sleeve is still out flat, then sew up the under-arm seams, stopping 2" above the cuff for the placket opening. If you can't find a pattern like this, see page 115 in <u>Mother Pletsch's Painless Sewing</u> book for a method of converting <u>any</u> sleeve to one with a back seam.

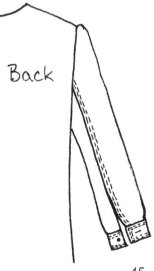

Back

Press back neck seam over roll to avoid seam mark – Hold down with Perky Bond – Can use wooden block to flatten.

COLLARS-----CONVENTIONAL METHOD

1. Cut the interfacing according to the upper collar pattern piece.
   To remove bulk, trim away 1/2" seam allowance so only 1/8"
   of the interfacing will be caught in the seam. Also snip the
   collar points diagonally to remove bulk.

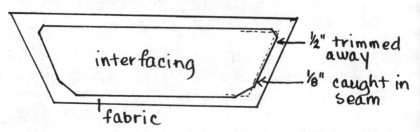

2. Fuse the interfacing to the upper collar, following the
   interfacing manufacturer's directions. Use a press cloth.
   (Fusible interfacings generally shape best when fused to
   the garment piece that shows: to the upper collar, to the
   upper cuff, to the garment front rather than the facing,
   unless that facing turns back into a lapel).

3. Assemble the collar according to the pattern directions. Be
   sure to understitch. It will help make a sharp edge.

4. PRESS WELL!

COLLARS WITH BAND-----FLAT METHOD

1. Cut two collar and two band pieces.

2. Trim 5/8" seam allowance from all band edges and from all
   but neck edge of collars.

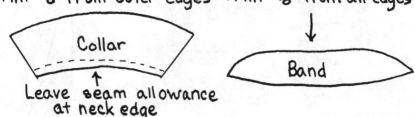

3. Cut the interfacing 1/4" smaller than band and collar. Where you left seam allowance on collar---only include 1/4" of interfacing in seam.

NOTE: Interfacing goes on upper collar and on both neck bands. It looks better, whether neck is buttoned or unbuttoned, if both bands are interfaced.

Mark center front on wrong side. Collar attaches here.

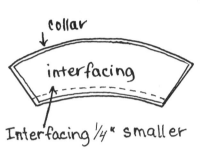

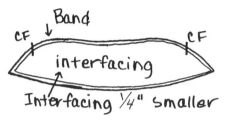

4. Staystitch the collar neck edge 1/2" from the edge. Clip to the staystitching line.

5. Overlap neck bands over collar pieces. Steam baste in place. Topstitch each separately.

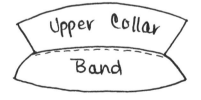

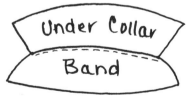

6. Key collar/band seams, wrong sides together, and pin so that bands will come out even at corners.

7. Staystitch neck edge.
   Place Talon Basting
   Tape 3/8" from edge
   on one or both sides.
   Clip around neck to
   staystitching. If not
   using Talon Basting
   Tape, lightly steam
   baste band to neck
   edge.

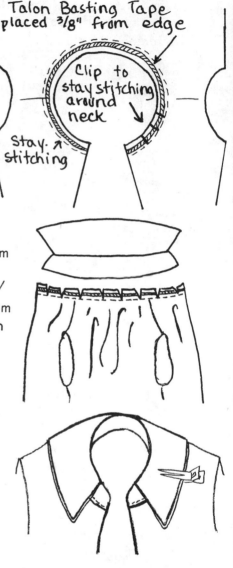

Talon Basting Tape
placed 3/8" from edge

Clip to
stay stitching
around
neck

Stay.
Stitching

8. Sandwich neck edge
   between lower edges of
   band next to stitching
   line. Stick, pin, or steam
   baste. Topstitch bands to
   neck edge. Unpin collar/
   band seam. Trim neck seam
   to 1/4", eliminating Talon
   Basting Tape.

9. Try garment on, or place
   it on a dress form or
   hanger to establish the
   accurate roll line for
   collar. If under collar
   slips out a bit due to
   the "turn of the cloth,"
   mark and snip away any
   excess fabric. Use
   hair clippies to hold
   collar edges together.

NOTE: Roll a linen dish
towel into a skinny sausage
and let the collars roll
over it.

Excess fabric trimmed away

48

10. Slip 1/4" strips of fusible web between collars and front edges; steam baste. Do not use Talon Basting Tape here, it cannot be removed after stitching.

Fusible web

11. Topstitch the collars and fronts together.

COLLAR WITHOUT BAND --- FLAT METHOD

When attaching a collar without a band we like the look of a conventional seam where the collar is attached to the neckline; however, a lapped seam may be used if you prefer.

1. Trim seam allowances from outside edges of upper and under collars. Trim away 5/8". Leave 5/8" at neck edge.

2. Cut interfacing 1/4" smaller and fuse to neck edge.

Collar

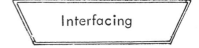

Interfacing

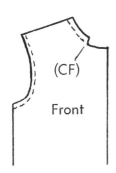

(CF)

Front

3. Trim 5/8" seams off front and neck edges of garment as suggested on page 31. Leave seam allowances on neck edge where collar will be attached. Collar comes to center front (CF) on most garments.

49

4. Trim 5/8" seam allowances off facing front and neck edges except where collar is to be attached. Attach neck facing to front facing at shoulder.

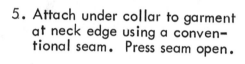

Staystitch neckline of facing and clip to staystitching to make it easier to sew to the straight edge of the collar.

Attach upper collar to facing at neck edge using a conventional seam. Press seam open.

5. Attach under collar to garment at neck edge using a conventional seam. Press seam open.

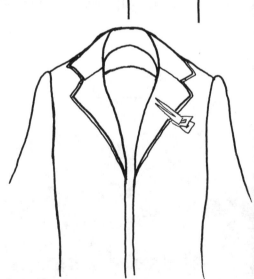

6. Place upper collar/ facing unit on garment with wrong sides together. Key neckline seams. Baste together. Trim upper collar/facing seam allowances to 3/8" and under collar/ garment seams to 1/4". Hold outside edges together with hair clippies.

7. Steam baste and topstitch collars and jacket front according to instructions on page 49 for band collar.

Blazers

A flat method blazer is constructed like a jacket with a convertible collar except for the following special techniques:

1. Trim seam allowances from outer edges of upper and under collar.

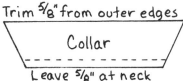

Trim ⅝" from outer edges

Collar

Leave ⅝" at neck

2. Trim interfacing 1/4" smaller and fuse to the under collar.

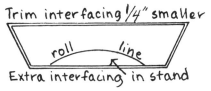

Trim interfacing ¼" smaller

roll line

Extra interfacing in stand

(For more body in stand of a tailored collar, fuse another strip of interfacing in the stand section just below the roll line.)

3. Trim the 5/8" seam allowance off the lapel and front edge.

4. Trim 1/2" off neck, shoulder and underarm of interfacing and 1/4" off front and lapel edges of garment. Fuse interfacing to front of garment.

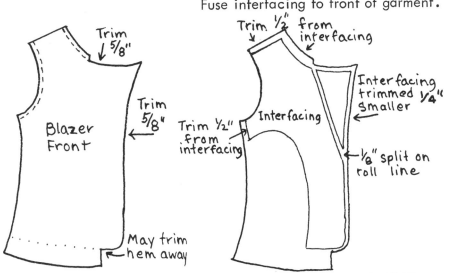

Trim ⅝"

Trim ⅝"

Blazer Front

May trim hem away

Trim ½" from interfacing

Trim ½" from interfacing

Interfacing

Interfacing trimmed ¼" smaller

⅛" split on roll line

NOTE: We found it difficult to get the lapels in Ultrasuede to lie flat. Susan discovered a neat trick. Split and separate fusible interfacing at the roll line leaving 1/8". Fold lapel at roll line and hand stitch 1/2" preshrunk twill tape over the roll line for added strength. Lapel will roll best if you pull tape tighter by 1/4".

5. Following techniques on page 50, attach upper collar to facings and under collar to garment using conventional seams.

51

Quick-lining

A quick way to line a flat method bazer or jacket...

1. Cut and assemble lining pieces according to pattern directions.

2. Stitch upper collar to front and neck facings.

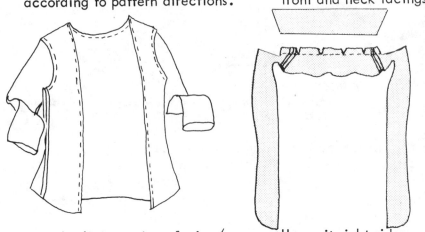

3. Pin the lining unit to facing/upper collar unit right sides together. Stitch 5/8" seams with lining side up next to presser foot, beginning and ending 1 1/2" from jacket bottor

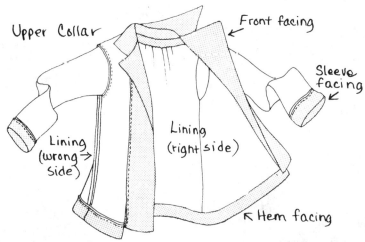

4. Cut Ultrasuede® facings for lower edge of sleeve and hem the width of the original hem turnup. Stitch to lining as show

5. Key neckline seams of lining unit to jacket unit wrong sides together. Baste. Tuck lining sleeve into garment sleeves wrot sides together. Match all raw edges of facings and garment Steam baste all edges. Topstitch all outside edges.

6. Hand tack lining sleeve seam around garment sleeve seam to anchor it in place.

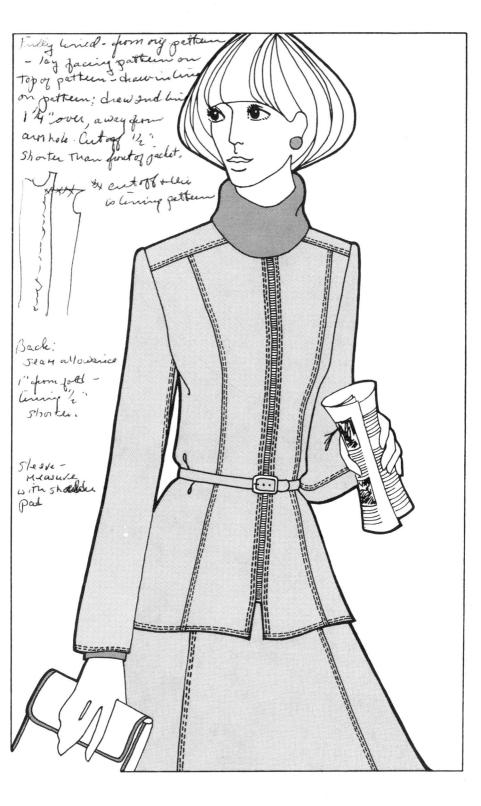

Zippers...Waistlines

CONVENTIONAL METHOD

Both regular and invisible zippers are suitable in conventionally done Ultrasuede® fabric garments. Susan made a
conventional blazer and used a hidden zipper in the pants in
order to carry out the rich, dressier look. Pati made pants with
a conventional fly front, since she prefers a conventional
crotch seam. See page 48 in Pants for Any Body, for an
easy fly front.

The following hints may be helpful for conventional method:
   1. Use a fusible web to flatten the overlap and underlap
      if you are doing a lapped zipper or a fly front.
   2. Use Talon Basting Tape to baste the zipper in place.

FLAT METHOD

EXPOSED APPLICATION

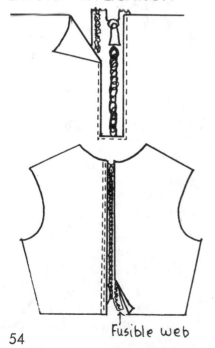

Fusible web

This type is great for pullover
tops or the bottom of a fitted
sleeve. Fuse Ultrasuede to
zipper and topstitch 1/8"
from edge.

Try a separating zipper in a
jacket front as illustrated on
page 53 . Fuse Ultrasuede®
to zipper. Topstitch 1/8" from
edge. Fuse facings to wrong
side. Topstitch 1/4" from edge
through all layers.

EASY CENTERED APPLICATION---FLAT METHOD

1. Omit the center back seam allowances entirely when cutting.

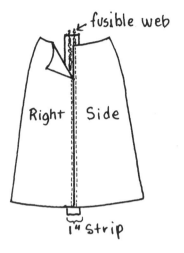

2. Slip a 1" wide strip of Ultrasuede® fabric under the center back seam edges and fuse in place with a 3/4" strip of fusible web.

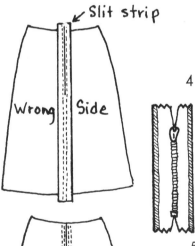

3. Topstitch 1/8" away from slit. Slit strip length of zipper opening. Center 1/2" transparent tape over slit on right side to keep slit closed while inserting zipper.

4. Place basting tape on the face of the zipper on both left and right edges. Peel away protective paper. Stick to skirt centering zipper over slit on wrong side with top stop 1" from top cut edge of skirt.

5. Topstitch 1/4" away from slit catching zipper in place.

LAPPED ZIPPER---FLAT METHOD

1. Prepare the zipper opening as follows:

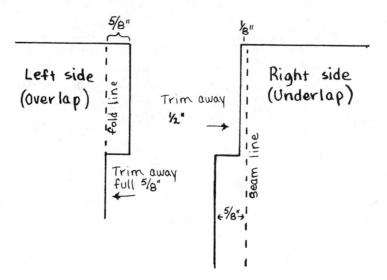

2. Place Talon Basting Tape on the face of the zipper to both the right and left sides. Peel the protective coating from the right side only. *doesn't need to be removed*

3. Put right side of skirt over right side of zipper. Stick in place. Topstitch next to the zipper coil.

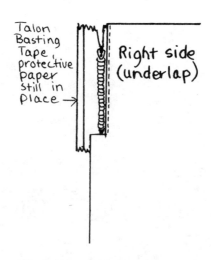

4. Fold under the 5/8" extension on left side. Fuse in place. Edge stitch the length of zipper opening. Pull thread to wrong side and knot.

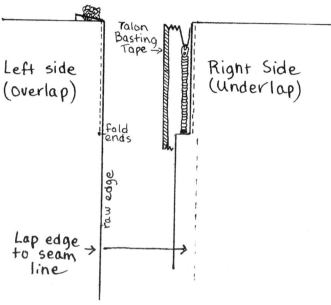

Talon Basting Tape →

Left side (Overlap)

Right Side (Underlap)

fold ends

raw edge

Lap edge to seam line →

5. Peel protective coating from remaining basting tape. Lap left over right in zipper area. Stick in place. Steam baste seam below zipper in place.

6. Topstitch full length of skirt 1/4" from edge. Then edge stitch rest of seam below zipper opening. Remove Talon Basting Tape.

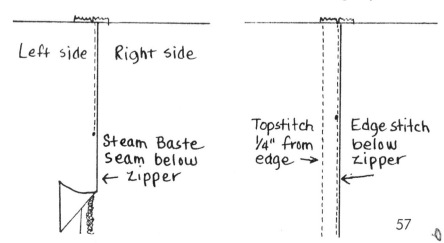

Left side ¦ Right side

Steam Baste Seam below ← Zipper

Topstitch 1/4" from edge →

Edge stitch below zipper ←

Waistband - Flat - seam allowance trimmed on front side.
Can be cut on crosswise. Measure at ease - + 2" for overlap.
2 x width + 5/8"

FACED WAISTLINE

CONVENTIONAL METHOD

1. Cut facings according to pattern pieces.

2. Fuse a lightweight fusible interfacing such as Fusible Pellon to the garment.

3. Attach facing to skirt or pant waistline according to pattern instructions.

4. Understitch to prevent rolling. Use your blind hemmer to understitch as it will be flatter. Lightly fuse the facing to the inside.

FLAT METHOD

1. Cut facings from pattern pieces. If pattern doesn't have facings, make your own:

Fold out darts.

Measure down 2" from top for facing pattern.

2"

fold

CB

2. Trim away the 5/8" waistline seam allowance. Leave 5/8" at the side seam on the back piece.

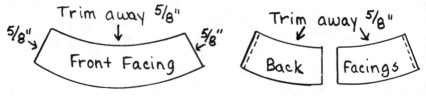

Trim away 5/8"

5/8"   5/8"

Front Facing

Trim away 5/8"

Back   Facings

58

3. Steam baste 1/4" preshrunk twill tape 1/8" away from waistline edge of skirt. Curve tape as you press to shape it.

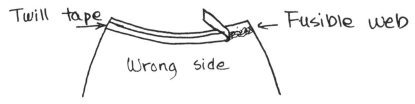

Twill tape

← Fusible web

Wrong side

4. Assemble skirt. Put in zipper.

5. Assemble facing by overlapping side seams and steam basting together. Topstitch.

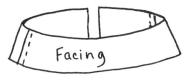

Facing

6. Fit facing inside waistline, matching seams. Steam baste in place and topstitch.

WAISTBANDS

CONVENTIONAL METHOD

We generally don't use a conventional waistband method on Ultrasuede® because the flat method is so easy. If you want a garment to be totally conventional in look, however, follow the instructions for our favorite method on page 40 of Pants for Any Body.

FLAT METHOD

We really like Armoflexxx waistband interfacing. It is a monofilament nylon waistband interfacing available by the yard in 1 1/4" to 2" widths. It doesn't roll, stretch or need to be preshrunk and is easy to use, lightweight and comfortable. Ban-rol is a similar product.

1. Cut Armoflexxx 1 1/2" longer than your waistline size.
2. Cut a strip of Ultrasuede 2" longer than your waist measurement, (this allows for a 1" overlap and a 1" underlap), and 2 times the width of the Armoflexxx plus 1/2".

59

3.  Wrap around your waist snugly and pinch together. Chalk mark where band meets. This would become the center front (CF) or center back (CB).

4.

	Waistband		
CB		CF	CB

Half way between center back markings is the center front. Mark with chalk.

5. Fuse Armoflexxx to wrong side of upper band with top edge next to foldline and other edge 1/4" from edge of band.

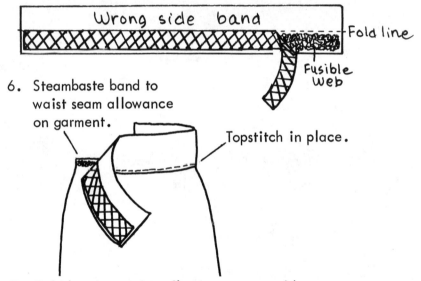

Wrong side band

Fold line

Fusible web

6. Steambaste band to waist seam allowance on garment.

Topstitch in place.

7. Fold band over Armoflexxx to wrong side. Steam baste in place to seam allowance of garment.

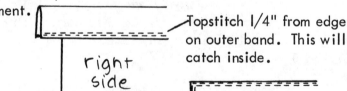

right side

Topstitch 1/4" from edge on outer band. This will catch inside.

8. Continue topstitching around ends and top of band.

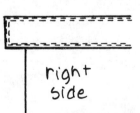

right side

Finishing Touches: Hems

HEMS--CONVENTIONAL

Hems are usually pressed up and fused in place for a dressier look

1. For straight hems, turn up a 1 - 1 1/2". Place a strip of fusible web the width of the hem minus 1/4". Fuse in place.

2. For shaped hems, partially ease out the fullness with machine gathering stitches. Place strip of fusible web in the hem to the fold. Steam baste first by pressing from the fold up to the top eased edge. Do not press over the top edge or you will leave an imprint on the right side. This type of hem should not be wider than 1 1/2". Any more would be too hard to ease in.

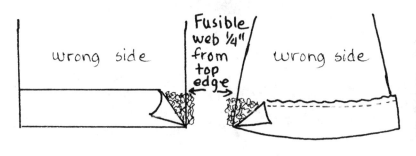

Straight hem   Shaped hem

HEMS---FLAT METHOD

There are two super ways to hem a garment made using the flat method:

1. The unfinished hem---Simply trim garment to the desired length and topstitch close to the edge to prevent stretch.

2. Faced hem---Simply cut a facing and fuse to the wrong side of hem edge. Topstitch lower edge.

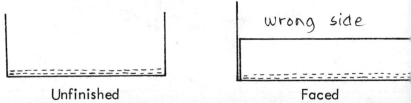

Unfinished   Faced

Buttonholes... Buttons

EASY, EASIER, EASIEST......(make samples of each method
first to see which you like best).

NOTE: Determine the length of the buttonhole by measuring the
length plus the width of the button. Test size by cutting a hole
that length in a scrap of Ultrasuede ® fabric and buttoning your
button through it.

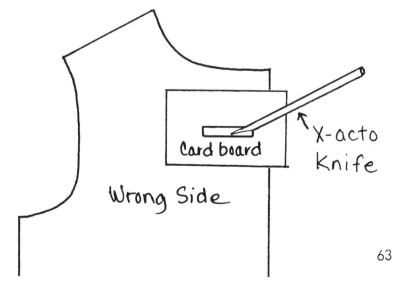

$\updownarrow$ width
plus
Length

EASY ---the topstitched window. See illustration on page 41.

1. Mark the location of the buttonholes on the wrong side
   of fabric with pencil or chalk.

2. Determine the buttonhole rectangle size and draw it on
   cardboard. Remember that a buttonhole is generally
   1/4" wide. Cut the rectangle out of the cardboard with
   an X-acto Knife. Throw away the rectangle. Place the
   cardboard over the buttonhole location. Using the hole
   in the cardboard as a guide, cut out a rectangle in
   the Ultrasuede ® fabric with the X-acto Knife.

Card board

X-acto
Knife

Wrong Side

3. Trim an additional 1/8" away from the interfacing on the wrong side to prevent it from showing. Fuse to fabric.

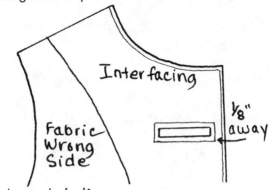

4. Make buttonhole lips:

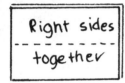

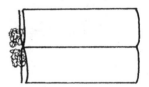

Cut 2 strips of fabric 1 1/2" wide and 1/2" longer than the buttonhole. Machine baste them together lengthwise.

Press lips open. Fuse.

5. Center lips under rectangle opening and steam baste with a fusible web. Topstitch around the rectangle to anchor permanently in place. Open basting between lips. (Topstitching may be done after facing is attached. Steam baste facing to back of buttonhole. Topstitch from right side throug all layers. Slit facing through buttonhole opening.)

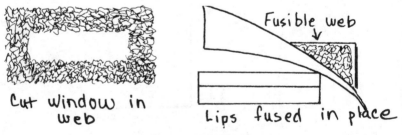

Cut window in web

Lips fused in place

Topstitch

EASIER---Machine Buttonholes

1. Make machine buttonholes through all thicknesses after the garment is completed. They look the best when an interfacing is used. NOTE: When using an interfacing with crosswise stretch (i.e. Easy Shaper or Pellon's T.D.) with a crosswise buttonhole, you will need to reinforce with additional patch of the interfacing going in the opposite direction before stitching to keep the buttonhole from stretching.

2. Slash open with an X-acto Knife. Place a pin in each end to prevent slicing the stitching.

EASIEST---A reinforced slash

1. After the garment is completed, determine the buttonhole size and location. Mark on the garment right side with chalk that will brush away.

2. Using 12-15 stitches per inch, stitch a rectangle 2-3 stitches wide and the desired length. Stitch around again over first stitching to reinforce.

3. Place a pin in each end to prevent slicing too far. Slash with an X-acto Knife.

4. Use a tweezer to pull out any stray interfacing threads.

SURPRISINGLY EASY --- a regular bound buttonhole

A patch method bound buttonhole done conventionally is super easy to make in Ultrasuede® fabric. It looks great!

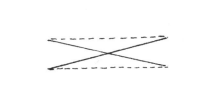

1. Place a rectangle of Ultrasuede® fabric over the buttonhole area on garment front, right sides together.

2. Simply stitch 2 rows the length of the buttonhole.

3. Slash from center to corners.

65

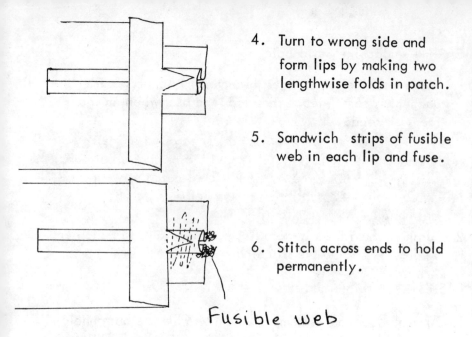

4. Turn to wrong side and form lips by making two lengthwise folds in patch.

5. Sandwich strips of fusible web in each lip and fuse.

6. Stitch across ends to hold permanently.

Fusible web

NOTE: To make opening in facing, cut rectangular shaped hole in facing same size as buttonhole. Fuse raw edges to back of buttonhole with fusible web.

BUTTONS

1. Stitch buttons on with polyester thread or with silk buttonhole twist, making sure to allow a thread shank if the button has none.

2. Use a clear plastic backing button for added strength.

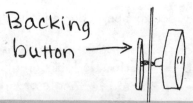

Backing button →

NOTE: You can make great covered buttons with Ultrasuede® fabric scraps. Use the one with the white rubber applicator. It is by far the easiest.

Pockets and Pocket Flaps

POCKETS

CONVENTIONAL METHOD

Use fusible interfacing on wrong side of pocket. Trim 1/2" off seam allowances of interfacing. Proceed according to pattern instructions.

FLAT METHOD UNLINED

Topstitch top edge of pocket. Steam baste outer edges of pocket to garment, and topstitch to garment.

Fusible web

NOTE: Fuse 1" circles of fusible interfacing to wrong side of garment at pocket stress points before stitching pocket in place.

NOTE: You may face top edge of pocket for extra body and strength such as for lower pockets that get lots of use.

wrong Side

FLAT METHOD LINED

1. Trim 5/8" seam allowance from pocket sides and bottom and 3/4" from lining. Sew lining to pocket at top. Fold over lining and steam baste together.

2. Topstitch across top of pocket.

3. Steam baste pocket to garment and topstitch sides and edges in place.

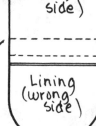

Pocket (wrong side)

Fold

Lining (wrong side)

POCKET FLAPS

Design your own shape if you like. Cut 2 flaps. Trim off all seam allowance and fuse wrong sides together. Topstitch sides and down edges. Steam baste, then topstitch top edge to garment.

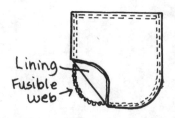

Lining
Fusible web

Creative Small Projects

If you are still a bit wary of tackling a pant suit or coat, here are some smaller investment ideas. Or...did you save those scraps? You may find that's all you will need for a super Ultrasuede® fabric gift creation.

ULTRASUEDE® FABRIC AS AN ACCENT

1. Use Ultrasuede® fabric as an accent fabric for part of a garment. Perhaps the front of a man's vest, or the front of a woman's jacket. It combines well with other washable fabrics such as polyester woven and knit fabrics, and is a beautiful accent on wool and wool knits too. Imagine how lovely a plaid pant suit would be with an Ultrasuede® fabric yoke, pocket, collar, and belt. Use the Flat Method. Simply steam baste the edges of a pocket or a yoke to your garment and topstitch in place.

2. Since it combines well with all fabrics, try it with a ready-made sweater or a sweater knit fabric as elbow patches, pockets or a belt. Simply covering buttons in scraps of Ultrasuede® fabric, piping a collar, and adding a belt can be a smashing way to change or update an existing garment.

Piping -- for bound buttonholes, piping a yoke, pockets, collar and belt. Cut 1" to 1 1/2" wide strips of Ultrasuede® fabric. Crosswise and bias have the most give if the piping is to be used on a shaped or curved area. Piping may be used flat--simply fold the strip in half right sides out, steam baste the raw edges together.

Corded piping -- place small string or cording (preshrunk) in the folded piping. Assemble your invisible zipper foot tunnel so the needle hits just next to the cord. Machine stitch.

invisible zipper foot

Ultrasuede®   cording

SMALL GIFT ITEMS

1. Sun glasses case: takes a 7" square.

      Fold a 7" square in half. Steam baste and topstitch bottom and long edge together. A decorative machine stitch is lovely here. Try metallic gold or silver thread in the machine top and bobbin -- a very elegant look. Tuck a small scrap of Ultrasuede® inside the case to use to clean your glasses. It's soft and won't scratch your lenses.

2. Foldover clutch bag: takes 2   9 x 12 Ultrasuede® rectangles and 2 7" zippers.

   ...In one piece cut two holes 7" long and 1/4" wide, placed as shown. Topstitch a zipper under each hole, stick in place with Talon Basting Tape. Stitch close to the edge with a zipper foot.

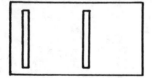

Topstitch zipper under openings

   ...Place both pieces wrong sides together. Topstitch through both pieces at the bag center. This will create two pockets and will allow the bag to fold in half more easily. Topstitch around bag to finish.

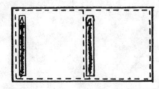

Topstitch through center.

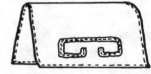

For a more decorative look, topstitch or applique a design before stitching together.

3. Brief case: takes 1/3 yd. fabric, one 14" zipper. For woman's case, purchase two wooden bangle bracelets for handles.

...Cut as shown.

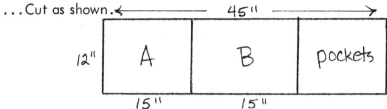

...Topstitch pockets on A if desired.

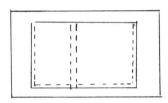 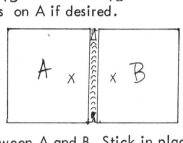

...Stitch zipper between A and B. Stick in place with Talon Basting Tape. Topstitch zipper under raw fabric edge. Remove tape. At the center and 2" down from the zipper at X, stitch on each bangle bracelet by inserting a 1" by 2" strip of fabric through the bracelet and topstitching the ends flat to the case.

...Steam baste and topstitch the remaining three sides.

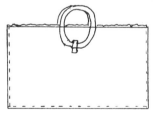

... Ideas for a man's brief case:

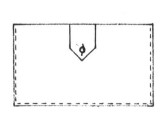 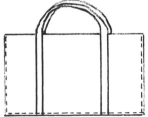

PATCHWORK

I. A super trim on a yoke and cuff or pocket, a great patched together bag or as an entire garment.

...Patches may be overlapped and topstitched as in flat method construction. Use either 1 or 2 rows of top-stitching.

...Patches may be over-lapped and decoratively topstitched together.

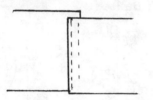

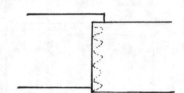

...Patches may be butted edge to edge and decoratively stitched together. Since this will not be quite as strong as the overlapped method, you may want to consider a backing for added strength.

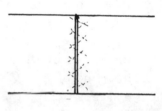

NOTE: Fuse all pieces of fabric to a pretty print backing fabric before stitching. This will hold all pieces in place for stitching and will eliminate lining.

QUILTING

A most elegant touch on Ultrasuede®. Fuse polyester fleece to the wrong side, then machine quilt. This can be used for a belt, a bag, yoke, cuff or pocket details, or as an entire garment.

ULTRASUEDE BELTS

Super Easy! Fuse 2 strips of Ultrasuede® together and topstitch for a soft belt. Fuse and topstitch Armoflexxx or belting between 2 pieces of Ultrasuede® for a firmer belt. Fold end around buckle and fuse or topstitch.

Sewing Menswear

Experiment with this thought---perhaps if your man could occasionally profit from your sewing, he might not complain so much about the amount of time, the amount of mess, the amount of money spent on sewing for you! Ultrasuede® fabric is really a natural for menswear---masculine, rugged looking, yet lightweight and functional. Since it tailors so well, it is beautiful for jackets, coats and sportcoats. Try some of the casual "safari jacket" patterns, they are super looking done with flat methods. One of the most magnificent sportcoats we've seen recently was a ready-to-wear coat of Ultrasuede® fabric.

For general menswear sewing information, we suggest the Simplicity Sewing for Men and Boys book or the Vogue Sewing Book revised edition. Men's Tailoring for the Home Sewer by Beverly Smith is also an excellent source.*

As in women's wear, use either conventional or flat methods, Armoflexxx waistband shaper, and flexible synthetic coil zippers. (Metal trouser zippers are not necessary).

Menswear is usually more structured than women's wear; the shape is more defined. One of the best menswear shaping products is the "Armo Jacket Packet" -- a kit containing all the professional tailoring supplies that are usually impossible to find separately. Armo also clearly explains how to use these supplies for the well-tailored look.

If you would prefer to begin with a smaller investment, a man's vest is a good project. Since the back is usually done in a lining fabric, that leaves only the front section in Ultrasuede® fabric---a quick and inexpensive, yet an impressive project.

Men's pants are just super looking in the Ultrasuede® fabric. Pants really personify that masculine, rugged character of the fabric--especially in a casual, jeans-cut pattern. We suggest making the pattern up first in another fabric so the man can really test the fit and feel of the pattern during extended wear. Fitting information for men's pants is included in our new revised Pants For Any Body.

We have included instructions for a new method of under-lining which we call "the combination lining/underlining method" below. Men are harder on pants, so it is essential to underline the crotch seam for added strength. The combination method does just that, but also gives a clean finished look to the legs.

We prefer to line both men's and women's Ultrasuede® pants to prevent them from sticking to the legs. Lining is a clean finish, but it doesn't add the same strength that under-lining provides. The problem is solved by combining the best of both techniques -- individually lining each leg and then joining them at the crotch seam so that you have an under-lined crotch.

Trust us! This method is rather difficult to visualize but follow the steps...completing each one before going on to the next...it works!

STEPS

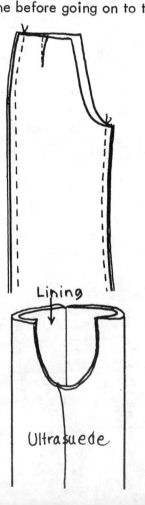

Lining

Ultrasuede

1. Sew darts separately in each Ultrasuede® and lining piece. Press.

2. Right sides together, stitch back and front pieces together at the side seams and inseams.

3. Do the same to the lining.

4. Place lining legs inside Ultrasuede® legs, wrong sides together. Each leg is now lined.

5. Turn one leg inside out and put the other leg inside it. Key inseams. Pin crotch seams together.

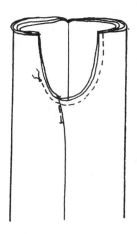

6. Stitch crotch seam to zipper opening.

7. Apply zipper and waist-band to lining and Ultrasuede®as one underlined unit.

Men's Tailoring For the Home Sewer by Beverly Smith may be ordered by sending $5.95 to P.O. Box 424, Woodenville, Washington 98072.

Love and Care for Ultrasuede® Fabric

Yes!!! You may machine wash and dry the finished garment providing you have preshrunk your findings---something not always done in ready-to-wear.

1. Machine wash (alone to avoid any color transfer from other fabrics) on a gentle cycle at warm setting, with a mild detergent. Use a cold rinse. Tumble dry at a moderate temperature. Don't overdry. Remove from dryer immediately

   NOTE: Best results in machine washing are obtained if your machine has a gentle agitation and a permanent press setting.

2. Handwash without squeezing. Soiled areas may be very lightly brushed with a soft-bristled brush. Hang to dry.

3. If necessary, steam press on a "low synthetic" setting with a gentle pressing motion. Always use a press cloth. Press on wrong side of fabric when possible. A terry cloth towel or another scrap of Ultrasuede® fabric can be used when pressing on the right side or maybe the new napped press cloth by June Tailor Inc.

4. Dry-cleaning should be done by conventional methods. We suggest having the garment dry-cleaned only and not pressed by the cleaners.

5. Store as you would any fine garment, on a padded or wooden hanger and in a closet bag or plastic cleaners bag. Fold pants and skirts over a doweled hanger to avoid clamp marks.

6. Stains - we have found that water soluble hair spray removes ballpoint pen ink and Spray 'n Wash® has been successful in removing grease stains. Cigarette burns can be scraped and brushed with a toothbrush to restore nap, but if serious, they may have to be cut out and patched.

"REINCARNATION OF ULTRASUEDE® FABRIC"

Occasionally, something we make goes out of style or gets sick (the cigarette burn fever?). What to do? We have seen mini-dresses cut off at the bustline and made into skirts with the remainder used to trim a wool jacket for a gorgeous coordinating outfit. Pants have been turned into a vest and too short coats become jackets.

Ultra's are indestructible!!

But Don't Stop Here!

We hope we have made sewing with Ultrasuede® fabric an enjoyable and fun experience for you. We have enjoyed the fabric and our garments for several years and are sure your time spent will have been a wise investment.

Now that you have joined the elite group of high fashion home sewers and designers who have worked with Ultrasuede® fabric, we hope you will try several more garments in this unique fabric. But most importantly, pat yourself on the back! You had the nerve and the fashion sense to try something new and different. Keep it up!

OTHER BOOKS BY THE AUTHORS:

Mother Pletsch's Painless Sewing with Pretty Pati's Perfect Pattern Primer, by Pati Palmer & Susan Pletsch. 136 pages of humor and hassle-free sewing tips. ISBN 0-935278-00-1. Copyright©1976. $4.50.

Pants for Any Body, by Pati Palmer & Susan Pletsch. 80 pages of easy-to-read instructions for fitting and sewing pants. ISBN 0-935278-02-8. Revised edition copyright©1976. $3.50.

Easy, Easier, Easiest Tailoring, by Pati Palmer & Susan Pletsch. Whether you have 35 hours for a beautiful "custom" tailored jacket or only 8 hours for the speediest, you'll find all the help you need in this 128 page book. ISBN 0-935278-03-6. Copyright©1977. $4.50.

If you cannot find the above books or additional copies of the Ultrasuede® book in your local fabric or department store, you may order them through Palmer/Pletsch Associates, P.O. Box 8422, Portland, Oregon 97207. Please add 75¢ for postage and handling.